The Adventures of Ariel and Ron

Life Lessons to Build One's Character

Dr. Dionne D. Nichols

Goose River Press
Waldoboro, Maine

Library of Congress Card Number: 2014902543

ISBN 13: 978-1-59713-191-9

First Printing, 2014

Artwork by India A. Perkins

Published by
Goose River Press
3400 Friendship Road
Waldoboro ME 04572
e-mail: gooseriverpress@roadrunner.com
www.gooseriverpress.com

Although Ron was the older cousin, he was the shortest in height. On the other hand, Ariel was the younger cousin, but was very tall for her age. So, they argued a lot over who was bigger.

Who's Bigger

Once upon a time, there were two cousins named Ariel and Ron. They were three years apart. Ron was the eldest and Ariel was the youngest.

DEDICATION

This book is dedicated to my niece, Ariel Henry and nephew, Rontez Hall, for your inspiration, love and support.

May God continue to bestow his divine favor upon your lives.

One day, both cousins were playing basketball in front of their grandmother's house and Ron decided to take the basketball away from Ariel and make several shots in the basketball goal. She became extremely angry! So angry, that she ran inside and locked Ron out of the house.

Ron then began knocking on the door and windows for Ariel to let him in. BAM, BAM, BAM, BAM! "Come on, Ariel, please let me in."

After minutes of knocking, Ariel finally decided to open the front door and let her older cousin in. Ron then said, "Just because you are bigger, I am still the oldest."

Both cousins hugged and apologized for making the other feel really small.

THE END

Lesson: Your height doesn't determine what's in your heart.

It's Boring!

One cold and rainy day, Ron and Ariel had to stay inside because the weather was too bad for them to go outside and play. Both cousins agreed that being inside was "BORING!"

They refused to take a nap. They refused to read a book and most of all they refused to do their chores. The only thing left to do was play video games. So, Ron pulled out his hand-held video game from his overnight bag and asked Ariel to play with him.

Each cousin took turns playing the video game. Ron earned a total of 1,500 points while Ariel only earned 300 points. The two began to fight over who was the best video game player.

Ron told Ariel that she can't win everything and she threw a big temper tantrum. The hand-held video game went flying across the room. Ron said, "Why did you do that?"

Ariel responded by saying, "You always win the game!"

Ariel began to cry and the "boo who's" became so loud that Ron felt really bad about beating her playing the game. So, he looked at her and said, "Please stop crying and let me show you how to play the video game."

The two cousins played the video game the rest of the day and forgot about how boring the day really was.

THE END

Lesson: Boredom develops a bond that can't be broken.

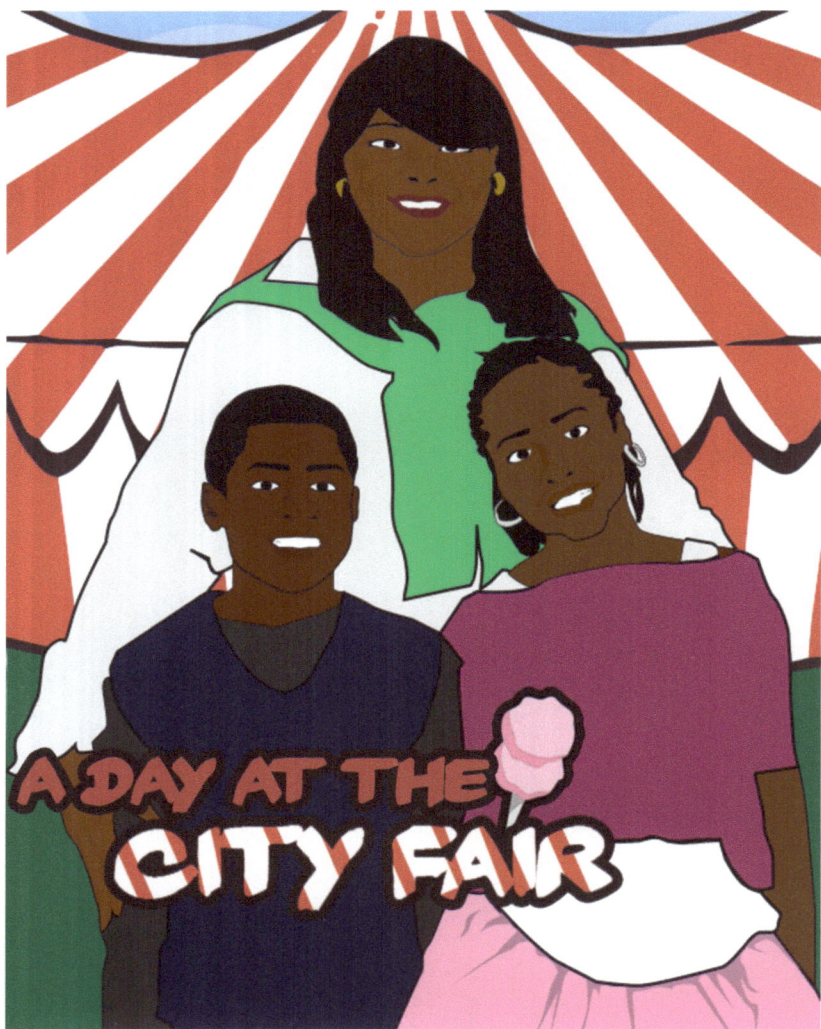

A DAY AT THE CITY FAIR

A Day at the City Fair

The City Fair came to town every year during the spring break vacation when students were out of school. However during spring break, Ron and Ariel convinced their Auntie Deedy to bring them to the City Fair.

There were many rides to go on, games to be played, food to eat, and sights to see. Ron and Ariel walked over to the big ticket booth and purchased their all day wristbands.

Ron wanted to ride on every amusement ride while Ariel wanted to play all of the games. So, the two decided to go their separate ways, but the plan was for them to stay together and meet up later by the bench where Auntie Deedy would be sitting.

Within minutes, Ron walked over to his Auntie Deedy and said, "They won't let me on the rides!"

His Auntie Deedy asked, "What do you mean, they won't let you on the rides?"

Ron explained that he needed to be over four feet tall to get on the adult adventurous rides.

Just then, Ariel passed by with a huge stuffed animal in her arms and said to Ron, "Why aren't you on the rides?"

Ron said with a very sad face, "They won't let me."

Ariel then handed Auntie Deedy her stuffed animal and turned to Ron and said, "We can get on the other rides together. Let's go!"

The two cousins walked off together and rode all of the City Fair rides that didn't have any height restrictions. They had an awesome time together!

THE END

*Lesson: Togetherness
is oneness.*

Sharing Is Caring

While walking from their grand-mother's house, Ron and Ariel saw a small, brown, stray dog that decided to follow them home. The dog appeared hungry and tired, but every step they made the dog continued to take the same steps and in the same direction.

As they made it to the front door, Ariel and Ron began to run to the front door very quickly trying to escape having the dog follow them in the house. When they slammed the door shut, the small, hungry and tired dog began to cry. He remained at the door crying until they let him in.

Ariel said, "My parents aren't going to let me have a pet."

Ron said, "We will keep him in the garage and take care of him and no one will ever know."

The two cousins took turns bringing the dog their leftovers and giving him water from the outside faucet.

A few days later, the dog decided to leave from out of the garage and head into the house. Ariel's mom was startled by the little creature! She wanted to know who let a dog into the house?

Meanwhile, Ron and Ariel were busy playing the blame game on each other. Ariel's mom reached down to pet the dog and said, "He is quite friendly."

At the same time, both cousins asked, "Can we keep him?"

Ariel's mom saw the excitement in both of the children's eyes and said, "Yes," but if someone claims the dog then we will have to return him to his original owner. However, Ariel's mom said in a serious tone, "The two of you will have to care for him." Ron and Ariel jumped for joy.

Weeks went by and no one came forth to claim the dog.

Both children went to Ariel's mom's bedroom and asked, "Can we keep the dog now?"

Ariel's mom raised up from a nap and said, "Yes, the two of you can keep the dog, but you will share the responsibility of caring for him."

Ron and Ariel named the dog Carter.

Ron and Ariel took turns feeding, bathing, and taking Carter for long walks around the neighborhood. He was now their best friend.

THE END

Lesson: Cooperation counts.

You Are My Friend, Too

Ron and Ariel were invited to a friend's birthday party. Before attending the party, they had to pick out a gift. While they were at the toy store, they had trouble deciding on which gift was the best one.

Ariel wanted to buy an MP3 player while Ron wanted to buy a Super Soaker water gun. The two tried to convince the other of why their gift was the best, but to no avail was either cousin hearing one another.

As they approached the check-out counter, a decision needed to be made. The MP3 player was chosen. Ron left the store upset.

When they arrived at the friend's party, Ron chose to leave Ariel all alone and he went off and played with the other guests.

Ariel felt sad and lonely. She couldn't believe that her cousin left her to go and hang out with other people that he did not even know, while she just sat by the pool and watched everyone play games.

On there way home, both Ron and Ariel were silent.

Auntie Deedy asked, "Did you guys have a great time?" and no one responded. The question was asked again and Ariel began to tell what happened. She said that Ron left her and she was alone.

Auntie Deedy began to scold Ron by telling him never to do that again! The two of you should never hold a grudge against one another. She then told him that Ariel is just not your cousin, but she is your friend, too!

THE END

Lesson: A family is a world created by friendship.

Don't Bully Me!

Saturday mornings are typical: Ariel and Ron eat cereal, watch cartoons until noon, and complete their chores before going outside to play. However, on this particular morning Ariel was up first while Ron was still trying to wake up. Ariel raced into the den to watch the Disney Channel.

Within minutes, Ron entered the den and grabbed the remote control from out of Ariel's hand. She began to yell, "Give it back, give it back, I said...give it back!"

Ron just kept clicking the remote from channel to channel while ignoring her request. The more he did that, the more upset Ariel became until finally she said, " I am tired of you bullying me!"

Ron looked at her with this sneaky look on his face as he took the remote control intentionally to make her upset. Just then, Ariel's dad came from out of the bedroom and asked, "What is all of the fuss about?"

Ariel began to cry, while stating, "He keeps bullying me and I am tired of it. If he's not taking the remote control from me, he is playing with my toys, and I am fed up."

Ariel's dad said, "There will be no bullying in this house. You two will either get along or stay away from one another. Futhermore, there is work that needs to be done around the house, so turn the TV off."

Just then, both children ran toward the remote control to turn the TV off and tripped over one another. They both seemed surprised at the incident, but within seconds began to laugh at how they made such a big thing over watching TV.

It was in that moment a compromise was made. Ron looked at Ariel and said, "How about we do our chores first and then do 'rock, paper, scissors' to see what channel we want to watch."

Ariel agreed and the two cousins watched the cartoon Nick Jr. the rest of the morning.

THE END

Lesson: Bullying is bad and unacceptable!

Dionne D. Nichols' Biography

Dionne D. Nichols is an educator with over 20 years of experience in elementary and secondary schools. She holds a Bachelor of Arts degree in Elementary Education, a Master of Arts degree in Teaching in Urban Schools and a Master of Education degree in Administration and Supervision. Most recently, she has earned her doctorate degree in Educational Leadership and Administration.

Dr. Nichols presently is employed with the Jefferson Parish Public School System in Louisiana as an Administrator in charge of Curriculum & Instruction. Her additional duties include: Title I, School Improvement and Parental Involvement. Dr. Nichols is committed to the idea of life-long learning, and believes that education is the key to success in life for both children and adults. More importantly, she is dedicated to leading change in our schools.

Dr. Nichols has been inspired by her niece and nephew's experiences and interactions to write short stories that depicts character building amongst minority children. Her hope is that every boy and girl be inspired by their experiences and to apply them into their lives.

Dr. Nichols is also the proud mother of her only daughter Shantrice S. Nichols.

www.ingramcontent.com/pod-product-compliance
Lightning Source LLC
Chambersburg PA
CBHW041955090426
42811CB00013B/1493

9 781597 131919